The Secret Life of Bees

by Sue Monk Kidd

A Study Guide by Ray Moore

Contents

Introduction

Plot Summary:

The narrative is set in South Carolina in 1964, the year in which the Civil Rights Act was passed. Lily Owens, who is just coming up to her fourteenth birthday, lives with her abusive father, T. Ray, on a peach farm. When Lily was only four, her mother died in circumstances that Lily cannot understand; she has largely been brought up by her black nanny Rosaleen. On the day that Rosaleen decides to go into town to register to vote, she is confronted by the full anger of white racism and the two end up in jail. Lily rescues Rosaleen from the hospital, and they begin a journey which Lily hopes will bring her answers to her questions about her mother.

Answers do come, but they are not always the ones Lily hoped for, and there is always the inevitability that T. Ray will find them both and attempt to force them to return to the peach farm...

Why Read this Book?

Upon publication, this first novel received critical acclaim and was on the New York Times bestseller list for two and a half years. It won the 2004 Book Sense Book of the Year Awards (Paperback), and in England was nominated for the Orange Broadband Prize for Fiction.

The strength of the novel is the primacy that it gives to women of strength and faith. Lily's struggle is really the struggle of an awkward girl to become a self-confident woman. All of this takes place against the background of the nation's struggle to live up to the ideals of equality on which it was founded.

Important: Issues with this Book.

The abuse that Lily suffers is physical, not sexual. The novel contains a few minor cuss words like 'shit-bucket,' and the word 'nigger' crops up a few times. This all adds to the novel's realism. (The 'n-word' also occurs once or twice in this study guide.)

Readers with strong religious views might be offended by the religion of the Boatwright sisters and the Daughters of Mary which involves venerating the Virgin Mary as a universal mother goddess. Lily comments that her own Baptist preacher and the Catholics would be equally outraged.

One of the main characters, the innocent May Boatwright, commits suicide by drowning herself. Her twin sister has also committed suicide before the start of the story.

A Note on the graphic organizers:

Two graphic organizers are provided to enable the students to make notes. Some simple guidance will be needed depending on how the teacher wants them to be used.

1

Dramatis Personæ:

The Owens Family and household:

Terrence Ray (T. Ray) Owens - Lily's father owns a peach farm outside of Sylvan in rural South Carolina (population 3,100). When he married Lily's mother, Deborah, he was passionately in love with her, but once she left him he became a bitter and resentful man. He punishes Lily so cruelly partly because he blames her for his wife's death and partly because she is a constant reminder of his failed marriage. (Lily looks just like her mother.)

Deborah Fontanel Owens - As a child, Deborah Fontanel grew up in Richmond, Virginia, where August Boatwright worked as her family's housekeeper. As a young woman, Deborah moved to Sylvan, following a friend from high school. She dated T. Ray and agreed to marry him after she discovered she was pregnant. At first, Deborah was in love with T. Ray and happy in her marriage, but she became depressed living in isolation on the farm and had trouble accepting the responsibilities of a mother. Before her death, Lily's mother had already left her husband and daughter Lily and gone to stay with her old housekeeper, August Boatwright, in the nearby town of Tiburon. On December 3, 1954, she returned to the Owens farm to pick up her clothes and take Lily away with her, but whilst she was there T. Ray returned. They got into a violent argument in the course of which Lily picked up a gun which went off killing her mother.

Lily Melissa Owens - The novel's protagonist and narrator is a fourteen-year-old white girl born on the Fourth of July in 1950. She was four when she accidentally shot her mother an action for which she feels tremendous guilt, though there are times when she wonders whether it really happened the way T. Ray has told her that it did. As Lily enters adolescence, she feels herself to be unattractive and unfeminine; she misses having a mother to guide her through the changes in her body (like her first period and her first training bra). Lily's most prized possessions are a few things of her mother's she found in her father's attic: a picture of Deborah, a wooden picture of a black Mary, and a pair of white gloves. They are like religious relics.

Rosaleen Daise - Lily's Negro nanny was born into a large family in McClellanville, South Carolina. She was married, but she kicked her husband out for cheating on her. Rosaleen originally worked as a peach picker on T. Ray's farm, but six months after Lily's mother died, T. Ray took her out of the fields and assigned her to taking care of Lily. She loves Lily and does everything she can to protect her from her father's anger. Proud and determined, if a little head-strong, Rosaleen stands up for herself, even in the face of violent, racist men like the three men in Sylvan who try to stop her from registering to vote.

Snout is T. Ray's dog to which he is devoted.

The White Community in Sylvan:

Mrs. Watson - She is T. Ray's near neighbor who looked after Lily for the three months that Deborah ran out on her marriage.

Mrs. Henry - Lily's school teacher realizes the girl's potential to do more than go to beauty school. She encourages Lily to pursue her interest in writing in order to begin a career as an author or teacher.

Brother Gerald - The Baptist minister of a House of Prayer Full Gospel Holiness Church in Sylvan which T. Ray and Lily attend. A firm supporter of racial segregation, he is self-righteous and petty lacking all Christian charity.

Franklin Posey - The violent ringleader of Rosaleen's attackers. T. Ray calls him, "'the meanest nigger-hater in Sylvan'" (38).

Avery Gatson ("Shoe - The policeman who arrests Lily and Rosaleen. He allows Rosaleen's attackers to beat her up when she is in the jail.

The Boatwright Family and Associates:

August Boatwright - The matriarch of the Boatwright family is a middle-aged black woman. August grew up in Virginia where she studied at a black college and became the housekeeper for the Fontanel family because she needed to earn money. She went on to become a teacher, but she moved to Tiburon to manage the *Black Madonna Honey Company* manufacturing honey and beeswax on a 28-acre farm she inherited from her grandmother. By selling bee products, she supports herself and sisters.

June Boatwright - The younger sister of August, she resented August becoming a housekeeper for a white family. June teaches history and English at the local colored high school, but her first love is music. She plays the cello to dying people at the hospital and in their homes. May tells Lily that she once was supposed to get married, but the groom, a man called Melvin Edwards, simply failed to show up and since then she has refused to consider marrying because of her fear of being hurt a second time. June initially finds it difficult to accept Lily because she is a connection to the world of white people from which June had tried to separate herself.

May Boatwright - The youngest surviving Boatwright sister, May once had a twin sister with whom she had a telepathic connection, but her twin died several years before the start of the novel. Since that time, she has become extremely sensitive to the cruelties in the world and prone to bouts of intense sorrow and depression.

April Boatwright - Following a racist incident, May's twin became depressed at the unfairness of the world. August tells Lily that, "'when she was fifteen, she took our father's shotgun and killed herself'" (97).

Neil - The principal of the high school at which June teaches is single though May tells Lily that he was married once. Neil is a very tall man who has been unsuccessfully courting June Boatwright for several years: she simply refuses to marry him. To be near to June he helps around the farm.

Zachary (Jach) Taylor - Zach, August's godson, helps with the bees to earn money for college, to run a car, and to be self-reliant. He is a junior at the black high school in Tiburon and plays football for the school team. However, he resents the stereotype that black men can only excel at sports; he is ambitious and hopes to be a lawyer. In this he is encouraged by local (white) lawyer Clayton Forrest.

Jachson - Jachson is a (black) friend of Zach's. His actions lead to Zach being arrested for something he did not do.

The Daughters of Mary - A group of African Americans (predominantly but not exclusively women) who have created their own religion, based around the Boatwright statue of the black Mary. They meet for worship in the Boatwright house: **Queenie, Violet, Lunelle, Cressie, Mabelee, Sugar-Girl**, and her husband **Otis Hill**.

The White Community in Tiburon:

Mr. Grady - The owner of the Frogmore Stew General Store and Restaurant, he tells Lily where the Boatwright house is.

Clayton Forrest - Tiburon's principal lawyer, an old friend of August's, takes an interest in Zach and encourages him to become a lawyer. He is a good friend of August's. His office is decorated with pictures of him with his daughter which has a big impact on Lily.

Becca Forrest - The daughter of Clayton, the lawyer. She is a year younger than Lily and eventually becomes her first school friend.

Miss Lacy - Lily thinks that Mr. Forrest's secretary looks about eighty years old. Conventionally racist, she is shocked to learn that Lily lives with black women, and only too happy to tell T. Ray where he can find Lily.

Judge Monroe - The Tiburon judge is out of town when Zach is arrested, which delays his release from jail.

Eddie Hazelwurst - The policeman in Tiburon who is disapproving and suspicious of Lily staying with the Boatwright sisters.

Willifred Merchant - Tiburon's most famous writer, she has received Pulitzer Prizes for her books on the deciduous trees of South Carolina. There is a Willifred Merchant day each year.

4

Genre:

Bildungsroman

A *Bildungsroman* tells the story (normally, though not exclusively, in the first person) of the growing up of a young, intelligent person who goes in search of answers to life's questions (including the biggest question of all: who he/she actually *is*) by gaining experience of the adult world from which they have been hitherto protected by their youth. The novel tells the story of the protagonist's adventures in the world and of the inner, psychological turmoil of his/her growth and development as a human being.

Examples of this genre: *Great Expectations* and *David Copperfield* by Charles Dickens, *Sons and Lovers* by D. H. Lawrence, *A Portrait of the Artist as a Young Man* by James Joyce, *The Catcher in the Rye* by J. D. Salinger, etc., etc..

Lily's main personal struggle is with coming to terms with her missing mother and developing as an independent woman regardless of this lack of a mothering influence. She comes not only to understand herself much better but also to understand the ways in which the society into which she was born is changing.

Magic (or Magical) Realism

Magic Realism sounds like an oxymoron. It is used to describe a literary genre that incorporates fantastic or mythical elements into otherwise realistic fiction. The term is associated especially with Latin American writers for whom the acceptance of magic in the rational world is central to their fiction. (See particularly the works of Gabriel García Márquez.)

The world of *The Secret Life of Bees* similarly incorporates magic in an otherwise realistically described twentieth century world. There is magic in the stories of the statue of the Black Madonna escaping every night from the chains placed around it by the white slave owner and returning to the praise house of the black slaves. There is magic in the coming of the bees to Lily's bedroom and their whispered message that she must leave - bees can't talk! There is magic in the redeeming love of the bees for Lily who finds mothers in the queen, in the black Madonna and in August just when she needs the support of a mother. All of these things are treated by the writer in such a matter-of-fact way that the reader scarcely recognizes the irrationality and certainly accepts that they are as real as is the honey that the Boatwright sisters sell to make a living. The result is that this novel creates a world of its own, a world which is at once recognizably part of the South during the overthrow of years of white privilege and yet isolated from the wider world by its own beliefs; in short, a world where magical things can happen.

Setting:

Rural South Carolina in the mid-1960s provides the setting for the narrative. This is the rural South where any intrusion into the way in which it orders itself is resented, at least by the white people. It is a beautiful place in which ugly things happen.

Themes:

Race Relations, Segregation, Racism
The story of Lily Owens' search for personal redemption is placed into the historical context of the summer of 1964 in the South. The summer of the Civil Rights Act, when black leaders such as Martin Luther King and Malcolm X were advocating (in very different ways) for an end to racism, was also a summer when many white Americans, particularly in the South, were violently opposing the end of segregation. In his 1963 Inaugural Address as Governor of Alabama, delivered January 14, George Wallace had stated adamantly, "I draw the line in the dust and toss the gauntlet before the feet of tyranny ... and I say ... segregation now, segregation tomorrow and segregation forever." [If you have never read this speech, you certainly *should*. It is available on the Internet.] In an April 1964 letter, Wallace wrote, "White and colored have lived together in the South for generations in peace and equanimity. They each prefer their own pattern of society, their own churches and their own schools—which history and experience have proven are best for best for both races."

Rosaleen works as a domestic housekeeper in the Owens' house, a typical role for a working black woman at the time. To Lily, Rosaleen is a surrogate mother whom she loves, but even Lily ultimately has to acknowledge the depth of her own prejudice against black people when she realizes that she always speaks *for* Rosaleen because she thinks that white people are inherently smarter than black people. Rosaleen's experience when she attempts to register to vote on the first day, under the Civil Rights Act, that she can shows that laws are easier to change than are people's prejudices.

Rosaleen is one of two black people who are put in jail without justification, Jach being the other. From Jach, Lily learns of the frustration that an intelligent young man feels when he is stereotyped as excelling only at sports because of his race. Her own relationship with Jach makes her aware that she too is restricted by racism in that interracial dating and marriage are strongly taboo. (Interracial marriage has only been legal throughout the U.S.A. since 1967 when The Supreme Court struck down anti-miscegenation laws as being unconstitutional)

Lily's experiences with the Boatwright sisters force Lily to examine her own prejudices. Up to this point, she has assumed that all black people are like Rosaleen, who is an uneducated laborer-turned-housekeeper with no 'manners.' At the pink house, for the first time, she sees black people (black *women*) who are cultured, exceptionally well mannered, and able to run a successful business. Additionally, she is shocked that June discriminates against her at least partly due to her skin color, and even more shocked to find herself sexually attracted to a black teenager. All three of these things she has never before even thought to be possible.

Without suggesting that the way forward will be easy either for individuals or for society as a whole, the novel ends with some hopeful developments. Zach decides to attend a white high school, and Lily and Becca openly associate with

Zach at school despite being called "'nigger lovers'" (301).

Independence, Dependence, Interdependence and the Power of Female Community

The first time Rosaleen goes to register to vote, as is her right under the Civil Rights Act, she ends up being arrested and subsequently beaten. The second time, she goes as part of the "'voter drive at the Negro high school'" (281), and ends up with a voter registration card. In the contrast between these two incidents, a major theme of the novel is illustrated.

The bees' hive demonstrates the importance of interdependence in nature. Each subset of bees has a different role within the hive from the queen down. When one of August's queens disappears, she has to replace it in order to save the hive because the remaining bees will lose their sense of purpose and begin to behave in unnatural, self-destructive ways; similarly, the queen depends upon her attendants to keep the hive clean. The difference with humans is that roles within human relationships and communities are fluid rather than genetically determined so that the dependent person can, in other circumstances, become the one on whom others depend. This is true of the relationship of Lily and Rosaleen though it takes Lily some time to see how much she *needs* Rosaleen.

Until she comes to Tiburon, Lily has never lived in a community. Without a mother, her life has been dominated by her bitter and abusive father, and she has been isolated at school without friends. More importantly, she has had no one with whom to share the experience of her physical maturation (e.g., the coming of her periods and wearing a training bra). The Boatwright sisters, and their friends the Daughters of Mary, provide Lily with a great example of a mutually supportive female community. Thus, Lily finds moments of solace when she is working with others whose values and beliefs she shares. The group combines to protect Rosaleen when she registers to vote and Lily when T. Ray turns up and threatens to take her back to Sylvan. Yet even within this group, there are limitations to the power of interdependence because life is difficult and dangerous. Just as queens die and hives can overheat, so neither August nor May can help June out of her depression at being jilted, and neither August not June can prevent May from finding the suffering in the world to be unbearable and ending her own life. Nevertheless, her life with the Boatwrights shows Lily how strong women support, care for, comfort, encourage, and love one another so that Lily starts to feel empowered as a woman as her body begins its transformation. By the end of the novel, Lily has begun to feel feminine and to enjoy her own body.

Ignorance and Knowledge, Uncertainty and Certainty

Thirteen-year-old Lily is haunted by one unanswered question: Did she, at the age of four, shoot and kill her own mother? Unfortunately for Lily, finding the answer to this question leads to other questions that are just as troubling: Why did her mother abandon Lily? Did her mother not love her? Lily soon discovers, as the SparkNotes Editors write that "The search for knowledge all too often

8

provides knowledge which perhaps had remained hidden for a reason, for this knowledge often brings sorrow."

Lily fills the vacuum in her knowledge by creating an idealized picture of Deborah as a loving mother who still watches over her. Rosaleen knows that the truth will shatter this image and that Lily will be hurt, but is unable to protect her. August also knows that the truth will hurt Lily and she does everything she can to prepare her and to give her time to adjust to it. Eventually, Lily has to accept that her mother *did* abandon her, although she also learns that Deborah regretted her decision and tried to come back for her. Less obvious, is the shattering of Lily's secret hope that, despite his cruelty to her, T. Ray actually *does* love her. This is why she calls him on the telephone from the lawyer's office, an action which results in an immediate rejection and which leads T. Ray to find her and crush her hopes in him.

Unlike May, who cannot cope with the knowledge of the evil and suffering in the world, Lily is finally able to accept that humans are complex and fallible. She accepts the truth about her mother, because she knows that she is surrounded by loving mothers, and she is able to accept the reality that, in a tragic accident, she shot her mother because she has learned that living one's life by looking backwards with regret is self-destructive.

In the end, this knowledge will enable both Lily and Zach to become the people they want to be. Instead of going to beauty school, Lily will go to college, and instead of playing professional football Zach will go to law school to enable him to be a 'kick-ass' lawyer fighting for civil rights.

The Importance of Storytelling

Lily loves to read and aspires to become a writer and a teacher of literature. T. Ray mocks her interest in books and does everything he can to prevent her from reading, for example by prohibiting her from taking books to the peach stand. In contrast, Lily's teacher, Mrs. Henry, tells her just how intelligent she is and encourages her. Similarly, Zach gives Lily a notebook in which she can record her thoughts and stories because he knows how important it is for her.

The narrative provides plenty of evidence of the importance of stories. August tells the story which generations of slaves repeated about the statue of Mary escaping each time she was placed in chains by the slave-owner. She also tells Lily stories to help her learn to love and trust. Lily misinterprets the story of the absent nun, Beatrix, whose place was taken by Mary until she decided to return to her convent. Lily believes that the story is meant to tell her that August knows she has run away and that she will eventually want to return. This is not, however, the purpose of this story which is designed to tell Lily to trust Mary to know what it is that she herself wants to do and that Mary will aid her in doing it.

There is Magic in the World

Bees do much more in the novel than provide a good income for the Boatwright sisters; they do much more than providing a model of interdependence that human society might do well to follow; they do much more than provide the epigram for each chapter. There is something mystical about bees in the story: from the very first page, they seem to guide Lily towards redemption because they love her. Thus, they come to her room to tell her that she should leave T. Ray's house. The picture of the Black Madonna points Lily toward the pink house in Tiburon where she will eventually learn the truth about her mother. In Tiburon, she lives in the honey house, where her own mother stayed, and, when she licks honey off his finger, she realizes that she is in love with Jach.

The bees are mystically connected with the statue of Mary in Chains, which is annually smothered in honey to help preserve the wood. Just as the queen bee is the mother of every bee in the hive, so the Virgin Mary is the mother of every human. Mary in Chains is the statue which, according to the oft-repeated slave story made its escape from the slave owner whenever he attempted to lock it away from his slaves. The power of religious belief (albeit unconventional religious belief) is strong enough to impact reality. This is a story in which the "universal feminine divine" (2) is an active force. We see this intervention at the end of the novel when Lily learns that her mother *did* love her because she gets the 'sign' for which she has been asking - a photograph showing mother and baby together. She also learns from August that, despite the loss of her mother, "she is loved by this Great Universal Mother" (Raub), by August, June, Rosaleen and the Daughters of Mary and even by the bees.

Life is not Easy

August tells Lily, "Most people don't have any idea about all the complicated life going on inside a hive. Bees have a secret life we don't know anything about" (148). This is also true of the humans in the story: as with a hive, everything looks pretty calm from the outside, but inside there is the constant battle for the survival of individuals and of the community. As Lily's favorite author, Thoreau wrote, "Most men lead lives of quiet desperation" (*Walden*).

Although it is perhaps not evident as one reads the novel, it is a story dominated by suffering: two suicides, an accidental shooting death, two unjust arrests, a woman in despair because she was jilted on her wedding day, a cruel father who seems to enjoy inflicting pain on Lily ... the list could go on.

As Raub correctly states, "Throughout the novel, all of the characters are forced to cope with difficulty. They cope with grief, discrimination, abuse, and physical pain. They all use different methods to cope, and no two characters take the same approach." There is a clear distinction, however, between those who try to cope alone and those who reach out to others, or at least who accept the help and support of others when it is offered.

T. Ray is the first and most obvious example of someone who internalizes his grief with the result that he becomes a bitter and mean man who takes out his anger and frustration on an innocent child. May likewise tries to cope alone whether it is by singing "Oh Susannah" or by going alone to her wailing wall. Perhaps she feels that no one else can understand the loss of her twin (her other-self) but her reaction makes her sisters feel powerless. June also cuts herself off from others after being jilted at her wedding in a desperate attempt to avoid being hurt again, but in doing so she causes pain to May, who sees her sister wasting her life, and to Neil, who loves her. It takes the suicide note from May to jolt her back into engagement with the world. After being thrown in jail, Jach is in danger of making the same mistake, but largely because of the support of those around him (August, Mr. Forrest, and Lily) he rightly decides to channel his anger by engaging with the world through getting an education and becoming a lawyer so that he can actually make the world better.

In her depression, Deborah is one of the few characters who instinctively seeks the help of people whom she knows love her. It is true that in her despair she focuses exclusively on herself and makes the terrible mistake of leaving her baby. However, after three months with the Boatwright sisters, she is strong enough to face her mistake and to try to rectify it. All of her life, Lily has been forced to cope with her problems alone since she has no mother, an abusive father and no school friends. It takes several weeks in the company of the Boatwright sisters before she finally takes out her repressed anger by throwing bottles of honey. In the calm that follows this outburst, she is ready to accept the support of August and to learn the full truth about who her mother was and who she herself is.

Study Guide:

This novel deserves to be read *reflectively*. The questions are *not* designed to test you but to help you to locate and to understand characters, plot, settings, issues, and themes in the text. They do not normally have simple answers, nor is there always one answer. Consider a range of possible interpretations - preferably by *discussing* the questions with others. Disagreement is to be encouraged!

Chapter One

The queen who is missing from the Owens family is, of course, Lily's dead mother. The name "Deborah" is a Hebrew for "bee." It is her absence that causes both T. Ray and Lily to exhibit signs of "queenlessness."

The story opens in early July, 1964, when Lily is about to turn fourteen.

The bees which Lily hears in the walls of her bedroom (1) clearly have importance - the title of the novel makes that clear. At first, it is not clear whether they are real or a figment of Lily's imagination.

There is a huge contrast between white and black religion in this chapter which extends beyond the obvious segregation of the churches. It is significant that some of those most vociferous in support of segregation attend Lily's church. The most enigmatic religious artifact is the picture of the Black Madonna which once belonged to Lily's mother (14). In fact, icons of a Black Madonna go back to medieval times.

Notes:

"Sophia Loren eyes" (9) - Sophia Loren (born 1934) was a very popular Italian movie actress noted for her stunning beauty.

"Mr. Khrushchev and his missiles" (20) - Nikita Khrushchev (1894-1971) was First Secretary of the Communist Party of the Soviet Union from 1953 to 1964. The Cold War (c.1947 - c.1991) between the U.S.A./Western Europe and the U.S.S.R./Communist Eastern Europe was a period of extreme political and military tension. At times (e.g., the Cuban Missile Crisis of 1962) it seemed inevitable that one side or the other would initiate an atomic war (19). The sort of drills and precautions described in this chapter were common (though they would have been completely ineffective as would shelters).

"the Civil Rights Act" (20) - This Act was signed into law by President Lyndon B. Johnson on July 2, 1964. Its full title was: "An act to enforce the constitutional right to vote, to confer jurisdiction upon the district courts of the United States of America to provide injunctive relief against discrimination in public accommodations, to authorize the Attorney General to institute suits to protect constitutional rights in public facilities and public education, to extend the Commission on Civil Rights, to prevent discrimination in federally assisted programs, to establish a Commission on Equal Employment Opportunity, and for other purposes." Effectively, this legislation marked the beginning of the end of the Jim Crow Laws, those statutes and ordinances established between 1874 and 1965 to enforce the separation of the white and black races in the American

South. It ended the unequal application of voter registration requirements which was common in the South (the so-called 'literacy tests' whose only purpose was to prevent black people from registering to vote) and racial segregation in schools (the so-called 'separate but equal' doctrine which had been overturned by the Supreme Court in the case of *Brown versus Board of Education of Topeka*, 1956), at the workplace and by facilities that served the general public (such as 'whites-only' and 'coloreds-only' restrooms, drinking fountains and restaurants).

"The $64,000 Question" *(20)* is the title of a television quiz show that ran from 1955 to1958. The title (which entered the language and is still used) describes the highest money prize.

"Martin Luther King" (21) - On June 11, 1964, Dr. Martin Luther King, who attended the signing of *The Civil Rights Act* in the White House, had been arrested for demanding service at a white-only restaurant the Monson Motor Lodge restaurant on the bayfront in St. Augustine, Florida (21). (It is still there and has a Facebook page!)

1. For a number of reasons (her youth at the time, her limited understanding of the relationship between her mother and her father, and the psychological trauma that she suffered), Lily's account of her mother's death is incomplete and unreliable. In addition, the reader is unclear as to the accuracy of T. Ray's version of events. Put together as complete an account of what happened as you can from the narrative.

2. Bringing up a daughter as a single father is no easy matter, but even so, T. Ray is no Atticus Finch (from *To Kill a Mockingbird*). How does he fail to be a father to Lily? Why does he behave as he does to his daughter?

3. In contrast, Rosaleen Daise is in many ways very like Calpurnia (the black nanny whom Atticus employs to take care of his children Scout and Jem). What are Rosaleen's feelings toward Lily?

4. Account for the different reactions of Rosaleen and Lily to President Johnson's announcement on television.

Chapter Two

Notes:

The Supremes (50) - This is the name of an all-black female singing quartet that recorded on Motown Records during the 1960s. The group was one of the first to achieve popularity across the racial divide. *Where Did Our Love Go?*, released in 1964, was their first number one hit remaining on the top of the *Billboard* chart for two weeks.

5. T. Ray adds some details to the story of the death of Lily's mother, although as mentioned above he is perhaps not an entirely reliable source. Add to your account of what you think actually happened.

6. The night of their escape, Lily and Rosaleen have a big argument down by the creek. Explain what sparks the argument.

Chapter Three

Notes:

"Walden Pond" (57) - *Walden; or, Life in the Woods* was written by Henry David Thoreau (1817-1842). It describes a period in his life when he built himself a cabin and lived along near Walden Pond outside of Concord.

The Baptist "five-part plan of salvation" (58) - Presumably this is based on these five core Baptist beliefs each of which conflicts with Catholic doctrine:

1). Jesus Christ is the head of the Church and should receive primary allegiance from the Christian Church.

2). The Holy Scriptures are authoritative in all matters of faith and Christian practice.

3). The Church is a fellowship of persons who have received by faith the new life of the Spirit and given witness to this faith in believer's baptism.

4). All believers have equal access to God through the one mediator, Jesus Christ, and are responsible to offer themselves in grateful service to Christ and their neighbors.

5). God has granted the liberty of conscience to everyone, and the Church therefore should be free from the control of the state. ("Five Baptist Principles" by Gary F. Zeolla)

Eleanor Roosevelt (57) - Anna Eleanor Roosevelt (1884 - 1962) was the wife of President Franklin D. Roosevelt: she was the First Lady from March 1933 to April 1945. Both she and her husband were controversial figures (particularly in the South) because of their supposed liberal views on matters such as race and employment.

"General Sherman" **(61)** - William Tecumseh Sherman (1820 - 1891) was a Civil War General. Near the end of the conflict, his "March to the Sea." involved devastating parts of the Carolinas and Georgia. His troops captured Savannah on December 21, 1864

"Fort Sumter" (65) was a sea fort located in Charleston Harbor, South Carolina, was occupied by the Army of the United States when, at 4:30 A.M. on April 12, 1861, 43 Confederate guns in a ring around Fort Sumter began the bombardment which began the Civil War.

"Castro's sister" (65) - Fidel Alejandro Castro Ruz (born 1926) led a revolution in Cuba (1956-9) which deposed the government of Cuban President Fulgencio Batista and established a single-party Communist dictatorship. Juanita Castro collaborated with the U.S. Central Intelligence Agency against her brother's rule in Cuba before going into exile in Miami in 1964. (Democtaticunderground.com)

"Malcolm X" (66) - Born Malcolm Little (1925 - 65), Malcolm changed his name when he became an American Muslim minister. On March 8, 1964, Malcolm X publicly announced his break from the Nation of Islam. He was a campaigner for the rights of black people, but where Dr. King advocated non-violent civil disobedience, Malcolm X and the Black Muslim movement advocated violence against what they perceived as the violence of racism.

14

"Saigon" (66) was the capital of South Vietnam.

7. Comment on the significance of the following description, "I pulled the wooden picture of Mary out of my bag and propped it against a tree trunk in order to study it properly. A ladybug had crawled up and sat on the Holy Mother's cheek, making the most perfect beauty mark on her" (58).

Chapter Four

Notes:
Pawley's Island (76) is in South Carolina, 70 miles north of Charleston and 25 miles south of Myrtle Beach. It is one of the oldest summer resorts on the East Coast.
Lost Diamond City (78) - Lily refers to seeing a movie of this title set in the Congo, Africa. This may have been the 1949 movie *Diamond City* set in the diamond fields of South Africa.
"Birmingham, Sep 15, four little angels dead" (80) - This refers to the bombing of the black 16th Street Baptist Church on Sunday, September 15, 1963. Four members of the Ku Klux Klan planted an explosive device beneath the front steps of the church. Four black girls were killed: Addie Mae Collins, Cynthia Wesley, Carole Robertson (each 14 years old) and Carol Denise McNair (11 years old).

In this chapter, Lily begins to become aware of the depth of her own prejudice against black people. She admits that her view of black women was that "they could be smart, but not as smart as me, me being white" (78). Lily has never seen such a strong, mutually supportive community of black women, successfully running their own business. August is evidently not only educated and intelligent but also cultured and refined.

8. Examine Lily's complex reaction to the sculpture of black Mary which, she feels smiles at her as if to say, "Lily Owens, I know you down to the core" (71).
9. Why does Lily lie about her past to August?
10. What explanation can you think of for the wall stuffed with slips of paper that Lily finds?

Chapter Five

Lily has an entirely new experience: for the first time in her life, she finds herself the object of racial prejudice. This makes here want to shout at June, "Excuse me, June Boatwright, but you don't even know me" (87). For a moment, Lily is so shocked that she even denies the possibility of a black person disrespecting a white person. Having overheard the quarrel between August and June, however, leads Lily to an important epiphany, "Piss was piss" (88). Her growing awareness of her own whiteness is placed in the context of the news which is full of examples of whites violently obstructing the Civil Rights Act.
The religion of the Boatwright sisters is markedly different from that of the Baptist Church which Lily attended as a child. Whilst the Baptists are exclusive,

rejecting Catholics on points of doctrine and blacks out of prejudice, the religion practiced in the Boatwright house is inclusive: it is an amalgam of different religions; it involves a variety of forms of worship, including dance; and it includes the white Lily (only June, whose reasons are personal, has any reservations about her taking part).

Lily desperately wants August to love her and keep her forever. August teaches Lily that the bee yard is a symbol for the world at large, and from her Lily learns rules of the yard and ultimately of the world, the most important of which is that "every little thing wants to be loved" (92).

Notes:

Walter Cronkite (88) (1916 - 2009) was an American broadcast journalist and anchorman for the CBS Evening News from 1962 to 1981. Because of his professionalism and integrity, he was referred to as the "most trusted man in America."

"integration parade in St. Augustine, Florida" (88) - 1964 was a year of demonstrations and counter-demonstrations in St. Augustine.

"Mr. Raines" (89) - I have been unable to trace this name, but the description fits the murder of Lt. Col. Lemuel Augustus Penn on July 11, 1964 in Madison County, Georgia nine days after passage of the Civil Rights Act. Penn was driving home when three KKK members (James Lackey, Cecil Myers and Howard Sims) drove alongside his car and shot him to death. In state court, the perpetrators were found not guilty by an all-white jury.

"'my father was an Orthodox Eclectic'" (90) - When August tells Lily this, she has no idea what it means, though she pretends to. August is making a contrast between her traditionalist Catholic mother and her father who combined a number of religious views in his faith.

11. The calendar sisters pray to a statue of black Mary which they call "'Our Lady of Chains'" (90). Lily can see no reason for this name. What reason(s) can you suggest?

Chapter Six

The theme of knowledge versus belief comes to the fore. Man is about to land a space vehicle on the moon and eventually to put a man on its surface thus shattering millennia of beliefs and superstitions. For Lily, the moon represents her vision of her mother as loving and protective. She knows that if she tells August the truth about why she is there, the moon might break loose and fall out of the sky destroyed by the truth.

Notes:

"Ranger 7" (114) transmitted over 4,300 photographs during the final 17 minutes of its flight before crashing into the surface of the moon (Wikipedia).

12. Explain why Lily faints during the religious service in the Boatwright home.

Chapter Seven

Lily's developing relationship with Zach awakens her sexual feelings (remember that she is only a few days past her fourteenth birthday) as well as renewing her ambitions to develop her mind and her creative potential. From the first moment she sees him, Lily finds Zack physically attractive - something that her upbringing has taught her to be impossible. Her feelings toward him demolish the remnants of the racism into which she was born and raised

August's reference to reading *Jane Eyre*, along with the story she told her earlier about Beatrix the runaway nun, leads Lily to feel as though August is sending her a message that she knows Lily's past. Lily is tempted to tell her the truth, but still lacks the courage to do so. She knows that she is living in a dreamworld at the Boatwrights' but she desperately wants it to go on for as long as possible.

June and Lily are parallel characters: each is haunted by something that happened in the past with which they cannot cope. Unable to face the truth about her mother, Lily has withdrawn into an idyllic dreamworld at the Boatwrights' while June, unable to face the prospect of a second rejection, is refusing to acknowledge her true feelings for Neil.

Notes:

"Fats Domino ... Elvis ... Miles Davis" (117) - Antoine "Fats" Domino, Jr. (born 1928) is an American pianist and singer-songwriter. He was the biggest black rock and roll singer of the 1950s. Elvis Aaron Presley (1935 - 1977) was an American singer who brought black rock and roll to a white audience. He, and other white performers who followed in him, were frequently accused of singing 'nigger music.' Miles Dewey Davis III (1926 - 1991) was an American jazz musician, trumpeter, bandleader, and composer. Jazz was another cross-over from the black to the white music audience.

"The Fugitive" (123) was a television series which ran from 1963 to 1967. Convicted of murdering his wife, Dr. Richard Kimble escapes and tries to track down the one-armed man he saw on the night of the murder and whom he believes to be the real murderer.

"Jane Eyre" (130) (1847) by Charlotte Bronte (130) tells the story of the orphaned Jane who eventually finds love with Mr. Rochester.

13. References to other works of literature in the novel are never arbitrary. Find out a little bit more about *The Fugitive* and *Jane Eyre* and explain their relevance to Lily's predicament.

Chapter Eight

Lily desperately clings onto the hope that, despite all evidence to the contrary, T. Ray does love her. That is why she calls him, but he fails her test. The letter she writes is her way of coping with the failed attempt to connect with her father. At the end of the chapter, Lily touches the statue of the black Mary's heart and proclaims that Mary as her mother - ironically, Lily, the motherless-child, has a knack of attaching herself to surrogate mothers. Through this action, Lily hopes to gain the strength the complete the last stage of her journey: having realized the truth about her father, she must now learn the truth about her mother.

Through August, Lily is learning about the secret life of bees - the many things that go on in a beehive unseen. Clearly, this symbolizes Lily's secret life which she keeps hidden from August and the secret life of her mother, Deborah, which has been hidden from her. However, Lily is learning that most everyone has secrets, some of which they share with others and some of which they bottle up inside.

Notes:

"The Black Madonna of Breznichar" (139) - There are many Black Madonnas around the world but Breznichar does not exist. Kidd bases the Breznichar cult of Madonna on other places in Europe where such a cult does exist.

"kamikaze planes" (151) - This literally means "divine" or "spirit wind" in Japanese. Towards the end of World War II, Japanese pilots would undertake suicide missions in which they would fly their explosive-filled planes into their targets (normally enemy ships).

"Jach Palance" (154) (1919 - 2006) was an exceptionally popular American movie actor. The reference in the novel is borrowed from fact. Palance, who had come, with his white wife, to visit relatives in Northport, was seen strolling around downtown Tuscaloosa, shaking hands and signing autographs for both blacks and whites. This was enough to spark rumors that he had come to town determined to break the color bar. On July 9, 1964, Palance went with his family to the old Druid Theater on Greensboro Avenue, Tuscaloosa. There Palance was harassed by a mob of white people (there was not a single black person in the theater) and although he and his children escaped safely, the result was a near-riot.

"Nat King Cole" (155) (1919 - 1965) was an American singer who enjoyed tremendous success in the 1940s and 50s. From 1956 to 1957 he hosted The Nat 'King' Cole Show, the first African American to headline a television show. Although critically acclaimed and very popular, it was cancelled after 30 shows for lack of a sponsor.

14. When Lily goes to tend to the hives with August, the bees fly out and cover her. The experience is so overwhelming that it takes her outside of immediate reality, though she does not faint. Clearly she is experiencing some kind of religious epiphany. Explain, as best you can, what you think she is experiencing at this moment.

15. After lunch, Zach goes to drop off honey at the office of Clayton Forrest, and Lily asks to go with him. Why does August hesitate before agreeing that she can go with Zach?

16. What is the immediate motivation for Lily's impulsive decision to ring her father?

Chapter Nine

Notes:
The Gulf of Tonkin Incident (166) took place on August 2 & 4, 1964. Supposedly, on each occasion North Vietnamese vessels opened fire on the USS Maddox in the Gulf. President Johnson responded by seeking powers which led to an escalation of the Vietnam War. It is now uncertain whether either of the alleged attacks actually happened.

The Columbia Civil Rights March, July 28, 1964 (166) appears to be fictional although on that day the Columbia Avenue Race Riots did occur.

"American Bandstand" (175) was a popular American music-performance television show that ran in various versions from 1952 to 1989 for most of which time it was hosted by Dick Clarke.

"Sam Cooke" (176) (1931 - 1964) was one of the most influential black singers of his generation. A popular recording artist, he worked for the Civil Rights Movement. He was shot and killed on December 11, 1964, in circumstances that remain unclear.

Ed Sullivan (185) (1901 - 1974) was an American television personality (185). *The Ed Sullivan Show* broadcast for 23 years from 1948 to 1971, giving TV spots to the most innovative performers in pop music including Elvis and The Beatles.

The notes above indicate that the chapter makes considerable use of foreshadowing: the references to Tonkin, Columbia and Cook all presage violence or even death. There is also the building heat in the chapter which foreshadows a storm: the fact that a bee stings Lily despite the fact that she is sending it love suggests that heat makes bees, and perhaps humans, act a bit crazy. August explains that, even when people take precautions and act out of love, bad things sometimes do happen, even in the safest, most positive communities: the first example of this will be Jach's arrest.

On the positive side, the hot weather leads to the water-fight which finally brings Lily and June together. Then, May tells Lily that she remembers a Deborah Fontanel and that she stayed out in the honey house for a while. This spurs Lily to tell August the truth, but circumstances conspire against her because August is talking to Sugar-Girl about a problem she is having with her husband.

At the end of the chapter May suffers two shocks. Firstly, she finds out about Jach being in prison when she talks with Zach's mother on the phone. Secondly, she realizes that her sisters have conspired to keep the bad news from her because they do not regard her as their equal.

17. What is the significance of the dream Lily has in which her mother is searching for her but has the legs of a roach coming out of her body?

18. Explain what May is going to do.

Chapter Ten

The reader may diagnose May as being manic depressive and trace that state to the post-traumatic stress of her twin's suicide, but this is to miss the deeper significance of the character. May carries the unbearable weight of the pain of the world, symbolized by the boulders that she hauls to raise her wall, and the burden ultimately leads to her suicide. Her life is a "blaze of love and anguish" (199). May instinctively knows that her inability to get over her sister's death keeps her living sisters focused on the past rather than on their futures: like Christ, May gives her life so that others may live.

The chapter is full of images of rebirth. Paradoxically, as August explains to Lily, "'Putting black cloths on the hives is for us [the living]. I do it to remind us that life gives way into death, and then death turns around and gives way into life'" (206). The seeds which the Daughters of Mary eat as they watch over May, and which they cast into her grave, are "called manna ... they wouldn't dream of sitting with the dead without eating seeds. Seeds kept the living from despair..." (207). Finally, May's suicide note ends with this injunction to her sisters and friends, "*It's my time to dies, and it's your time to live. Don't mess it up*" (210). It is August who flat out tells June that ever since her disappointment she has been only "'halfway living'" her life (211).

At May's wake, Sugar-Girl makes a joke about the way bodies are views at "white people's funeral homes" (208). This is a turning point for Lily because she realizes that Sugar-Girl regards her as part of the group and does not see her as being white. This changes Lily's perspective: she no longer things of white people and black people getting along but of a society in which there are just people without reference to pigmentation.

Notes:

"Aristaeus" (206) was a minor Greek god of god of shepherds and cheese-making, bee-keeping, honey, honey-mead, olive growing, and medicinal herbs.

19. As August, Rosaleen and Lily search for May, the following simile is used to describe them,
"we must have seemed to the night creatures like one big organism with six legs" (190-1). Analyze the meaning of this image.

20. When May's body has been discovered, Lily thinks of August and June, "This had been the thing they'd been waiting for half their lives without even realizing it" (194). Explain what Lily means by this.

Chapter Eleven

Notes:

The "Malcolm X, and the Afro-American Unity Group" (216) - "The Organization of Afro-American Unity (OAAU) was founded by Malcolm X and other black nationalist leaders on June 24, 1964 in Harlem, New York. Formed shortly after his break with the Nation of Islam, the OAAU was a secular institution that sought to unify 22 million non-Muslim African Americans with the people of the African Continent" (blackpast.org).

The religious service which the Daughters of Mary share on Mary Day takes elements of several faiths, but would be regarded as equally blasphemous by the Baptists and the Catholics. This predominantly female group is reasserting the belief in God as Universal Mother which pre-dates Christianity.

Jach has been hardened by his experience of being arrested for something that he did not do. Lily hopes that he will not become mean, but he assures her that he will channel his anger into his studies and that he will build a world in which mixed-race couples can be together.

21. The chapter ends with Lily reflecting, "Wading in up to my neck" (231). This is a reference back to her failure of courage when the boys tied dying fish around her neck. Explain how Lily has changed since the two incidents and precisely what she means in that sentence.

Chapter Twelve

The novel reaches its climax as Lily begins to find the answers to the questions she has always had about her mother. Lily learns from August that Deborah actually did abandon her, and this shatters her unrealistic idealized image of her loving mother, even though she learns that after three months with the Boatwrights Deborah returned to Sylvan to fetch her. Lily must now learn to live with the knowledge that Deborah was a human being, imperfect, and, like all humans (indeed like most of the characters in the novel), capable of making mistakes.

A modern psychologist might diagnose Deborah as suffering from postpartum depression the symptoms of which "may include sadness, low energy, changes in sleeping and eating patterns, reduced desire for sex, crying episodes, anxiety, and irritability" (Wikipedia).

22. How was Deborah's future unhappiness as an adult (particularly as a wife and mother) prefigured by the kind of child she was?

Chapter Thirteen

Rosaleen's decision not to tell Lily the truth about her mother parallels August's decision not to tell May about Jach's arrest. Both acts spring from a desire to protect a loved person, but each is counterproductive. In Lily's case, she has invested so much in the myth of her loving mother that she cannot handle the truth. She reacts with anger against the world: an anger which could potentially develop into the same bitterness that has ruined T. Ray's life. Just like Jach's anger at being thrown in jail, Lily's anger has the power to be self-destructive.

Lily reacts violently to hearing the truth about Deborah by smashing the honey jars against the wall. Angry at her mother, Lily lashes out at the world, much as T. Ray did throughout her childhood, except that he focused his meanness on the daughter who was a constant reminder of the wife who had deserted him and then been killed.

23. August gives Lily a picture of herself as a child in the arms of her mother. Explain the full significance that this photograph has for Lily.

Chapter Fourteen

Notes:

"'casting my vote for Mr. Johnson'" (283) - The presidential election of 1964 was held on Tuesday, November 3. The Democratic candidate was sitting President Lyndon Johnson (with vice-presidential candidate Hubert Humphrey) and the Republican candidate was Senator Barr Goldwater (with vice-presidential candidate William Miller). Johnson was elected carrying 44 of the 50 states and the District of Columbia and winning 61% of the popular vote.

Victories are won in this chapter. June finally marries Neil, Jach finds the courage to desegregate a white high school, Lily gets her first true school friend, and Rosaleen successfully registers to vote, largely because she does not try to take on the system all alone. Lily learns to live her life forwards instead of always harping on the past and that she is not motherless. This gives her the strength to stand up to T. Ray, though again it is the community of the Daughters of Mary, and particularly August who give her the power to do so. More than this, she realizes that he too has suffered because of the loss of the wife he loved just as she has suffered for the loss of her mother. She even has the strength to face the probability that she was holding the gun when it went off and killed her mother. Nevertheless, T. Ray cannot respond to being called 'Daddy' by his daughter (although the word does bring him back to reality and remind him that he is talking to Lily not to Deborah): some hurts are too deep and too damaging ever to heal.

24. Lily takes particular care of a set of mouse bones, though she says that she does not really understand why. Suggest what the significance of the bones may be.

25. Explain the full significance of the whale pin to: a) T. Ray, and b) Lily.

26. Did Lily shoot Deborah? Explain your answer.

Glossary
Literary terms you will find useful in discussing this novel

first-person narrator/narrative - The narrative in a work of fiction may either be third or first person. Third person narrative is told by an unidentified voice which belongs to someone not directly involved in the events narrated. First person narrative means that story is told from the necessarily limited viewpoint of one of the characters writing or speaking directly about themselves and their experience.

foreshadowing - An author uses foreshadowing when he/she hints at a future development in the plot. This builds up the reader's involvement in the fiction.

image - Imagery is a blanket term that describes the use of figurative language to represent objects, actions and ideas in such a way that it appeals to our five physical senses. Thus, amongst others, similes, metaphors and symbolism are examples of images.

 metaphor - A metaphor is a implied comparison in which whatever is being described is referred to as though it were another thing (e.g., "To be, or not to be: that is the question: / Whether 'tis nobler in the mind to suffer / The slings and arrows of outrageous fortune, / Or to take arms against a sea of troubles, / And by opposing end them?" Shakespeare Hamlet)

 simile - A simile is a descriptive comparison which uses the words "like" or "as" to make the intended comparison clear (e.g., "O my Luve's like a red, red rose / That's newly sprung in June; / O my Luve's like the melodie / That's sweetly play'd in tune." Robert Burns).

 symbol - A description in which one thing stands for or represents or suggests something bigger and more significant than itself. Normally a material object is used to represent an idea, belief, action, theme, person, etc. (e.g., in the Burns poem above, he uses the rose because it is a traditional symbol for love, passion, emotion and romance just as the sun became a natural and almost universal symbol of kingship).

irony / ironic - The essential feature of irony is the presence of a contradiction between an action or expression and the meaning it has in the context in which it occurs. Writers are always conscious of using irony, but there characters may either be aware or unaware that something that they say or do is ironic. Dramatic irony is the term used to describe a character saying or doing something that has significance for the audience or reader but of which the characters are not aware. For example, when Othello says, "If it were now to die, / 'Twere now to be most happy, for I fear / My soul hath her content so absolute / That not another comfort like to this / Succeeds in unknown fate" (*Othello* 2:1), this is dramatic irony because the audience knows that he speaks truer than he knows.

motivation - Since Sigmund Freud 'invented' psychoanalysis, motivation has predominantly been though or in terms of psychology. Thus, the actions of a character may surprise us but they should also strike us as psychologically plausible.

oxymoron - This is a phrase in which in which two opposite ideas are joined to create an effect (e.g., you have to be cruel to be kind; an open secret; etc.).

stereotype - An oversimplified generalization used to describe or define a social group, or individuals from a group (e.g., the title of the movie *White Men Can't Jump*).

Further Reading

Bastard Out of Carolina by Dorothy Allison gives a convincing portrait of the lives of 'poor white trash.' The setting, in terms of time and place, is very similar to *The Secret Life of Bees*.

Chains: Seeds of America by Laurie Halse Anderson is a historical novel set in 1776. It is written for younger teens, but I found it a very satisfying read. Its protagonist is thirteen-year-old slave Isabel.

Go Set a Watchman by Harper Lee tell the story of the adult Scout (Jean Louise Finch) returning home for a summer vacation when she is 26. It describes the shattering discovery by the adult Scout that her beloved father, Atticus Finch, holds racist views and believes in segregation.

The Invention of Wings by Sue Monk Kidd tells the story of two women, one white and one black, woman who, in their different ways, fight against slavery and racism in nineteenth century Charleston.

The Help by Kathryn Stockett tells the story of house black maids like Rosaleen and Calpurnia in white households in Jackson, Mississippi, during the early 1960s.

To Kill a Mockingbird by Harper Lee tells of Atticus Finch defending a black man accused of raping a white girl. The story is told from the perspective of Atticus' daughter Jean Louise (Scout) Finch.

Works Cited

Kidd, Sue Monk. *The Secret Life of Bees*. New York: Penguin, 2003. Print.

SparkNotes Editors. "SparkNote on The Secret Life of Bees." SparkNotes.com. SparkNotes LLC. 2006. Web. 20 Aug. 2015.

Raub, Adena. Kissel, Adam ed. *"The Secret Life of Bees* Study Guide." GradeSaver, 30 November 2008. Web. 3 September 2015.

VOCABULARY

How do we learn new words?

In the first four years of your life you learned more words than you will learn in the rest of your life! You did this by listening to other people speak. Simply by hearing a word over and over again, you worked out what it meant. (That is why most babies say the words 'mommy' or 'daddy' first.)

As we get older, we still use this method to learn new words, but it does not work so well. That is because the words that we still do not know tend not to come up too often, so we do not get that repetition that helps us to work out what the words mean. (How many times are you likely to come across the word 'increments' in the next month? It is in this novel, but you are unlikely to hear or read it again for a while!)

As a result, we have to make a deliberate effort to learn new words. Here is the best way:

1. When you first see the word, try to relate it to other words that you already know. For example, 'mysticism' sounds like 'mystery' which means 'a puzzle, something unusual which does not have an obvious solution.'

2. Look at the word in context. If you are able to relate it to a word that you know, does this meaning make any sense? Does the context add to your understanding of what the new word means? If you are unable to relate the word to one that you already knew, try reading the sentence with a blank where the new word goes. Ask yourself what word or phrase would you put into the blank to make sense in this context. Put your thoughts and guesses on the first line.

3. Check the dictionary definition of the word. Remember that every word has a range of meanings. You need to know what the word means in the context in which it is used.

Vocabulary Activity

1. presumptuous, adj. (2)   *Forward, over-familiar, arrogant, pushy.*

2. oblivious, adj. (21)   *Unaware, preoccupied, not seeing or hearing.*

3. recoil, verb (32)   *To start or jump back from, to flinch or retreat from.*

4. brazen, adj. (38)   *Brash, bold, immodest, impolite, audacious.*

5. consternation, noun (64)   *Fear, concern, worry.*

6. meander, verb (80)   _____

7. naïve, adj. (84)   _____

8. indignation, noun (87)   _____

9. ingenious, adj. (104)   _____

10. incessantly, adj. (120)   _____

11. anguish, noun (199)   _____

12. induction, noun (206)   _____

13. sauntered, verb (224)   _____

14. demoralized, verb (286)   _____

15. resolve, verb (298)   _____

16. perpetually, adj. (301)   _____

VOCABULARY TEST

Below are some sentences. Select the word(s) from the vocabulary list that fits into each sentence. Some may be used more than once; some may not be used.

presumptuous	oblivious	recoil	brazen	consternation
meander	naïve	indignation	ingenious	incessantly
anguish	induction	sauntered	demoralized	resolve
perpetually				

a) The _____ from the rifle shot just about broke my shoulder.

b) Following very poor reviews of his latest book, the writer felt _____ against the critics who had slammed it.

c) The teacher was a little _____ to believe that all of the students would hand in the work on time; her optimism was misplaced.

d) The home run that Adam hit in the fifth innings scored a triple leaving the opposing team completely _____.

e) The policeman suspected that the driver was drunk when his car began to _____ across all three lanes of the highway.

f) It was rather _____ of Romeo to climbs up to Juliet's balcony, but he was in love.

g) The flame at the grave of President John F. Kennedy burns _____.

h) There had been no rain for years, and then it rained _____ for three weeks.

i) The coach, a former professional, demanded more _____ and determination from the players at the tennis academy.

j) The teacher appeared to be _____ to the taunting and bullying that went on in his classroom.

k) The proposed _____ of Pete Rose into the Baseball Hall of Fame was once again defeated.

l) At the talent show, Rory _____ up to the microphone as though he had no nerves at all.

m) The kicker watched with mounting _____ as the game-winning conversion went wide.

n) The supposed relic was in face a forgery which the archeologist was
_____ enough to present as genuine.

o) On the final lap of the one mile race, Roy's _____ finally
evaporated as Katie blew past him in the back stretch.

p) The plan was certainly _____ - perhaps it was just a little too
clever.

Appendix 1: Classroom Use of the Study Guide Questions

Although there are both closed and open questions in the Study Guide, very few of them have simple, right or wrong answers. They are designed to encourage in-depth discussion, disagreement, and (eventually) consensus. Above all, they aim to encourage students to go to the text to support their conclusions and interpretations.

I am not so arrogant as to presume to tell teachers how they should use this resource. I used it in the following ways, each of which ensured that students were well prepared for class discussion and presentations.

1. Set a reading assignment for the class and tell everyone to be aware that the questions will be the focus of whole class discussion the next class.

2. Set a reading assignment for the class and allocate particular questions to sections of the class (e.g. if there are four questions, divide the class into four sections, etc.).

In class, form discussion groups containing one person who has prepared each question and allow time for feedback within the groups.

Have feedback to the whole class on each question by picking a group at random to present their answers and to follow up with class discussion.

3. Set a reading assignment for the class, but do not allocate questions.

In class, divide students into groups and allocate to each group one of the questions related to the reading assignment the answer to which they will have to present formally to the class.

Allow time for discussion and preparation.

4. Set a reading assignment for the class, but do not allocate questions.

In class, divide students into groups and allocate to each group one of the questions related to the reading assignment.

Allow time for discussion and preparation.

Now reconfigure the groups so that each group contains at least one person who has prepared each question and allow time for feedback within the groups.

5. Before starting to read the text, allocate specific questions to individuals or pairs. (It is best not to allocate all questions to allow for other approaches and variety. One in three questions or one in four seems about right.) Tell students that they will be leading the class discussion on their question. They will need to start with a brief presentation of the issues and then conduct a question and answer session. After this, they will be expected to present a brief review of the discussion.

6. Having finished the text, arrange the class into groups of 3, 4 or 5. Tell each group to select as many questions from the Study Guide as there are members of the group.

Each individual is responsible for drafting out a written answer to one question, and each answer should be a substantial paragraph.

Each group as a whole is then responsible for discussing, editing and suggesting improvements to each answer, which is revised by the original writer and brought back to the group for a final proof reading followed by revision.

This seems to work best when the group knows that at least some of the points for the activity will be based on the quality of all of the answers.

Graphic organizers

Plot graph for *The Secret Life of Bees*

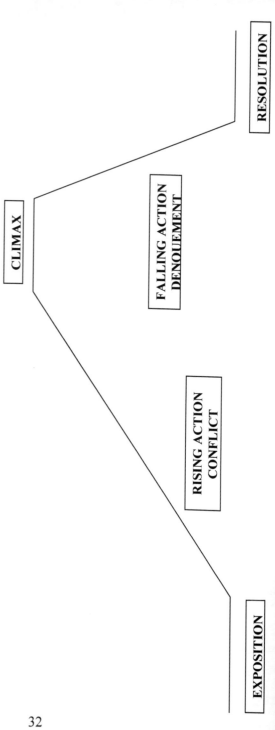

EXPOSITION

RISING ACTION
CONFLICT

CLIMAX

FALLING ACTION
DENOUEMENT

RESOLUTION

Developing perspectives on the situation which initiates the action in the novel

Deborah

Lily

August

Deborah leaves her husband and her child

T.Ray

VOCABULARY TEST: ANSWERS

presumptuous	oblivious	recoil	brazen	consternation
meander	naïve	indignation	ingenious	incessantly
anguish	induction	sauntered	demoralized	resolve
perpetually				

a) The **recoil** from the rifle shot just about broke my shoulder.

b) Following very poor reviews of his latest book, the writer felt **indignation** against the critics who had slammed it.

c) The teacher was a little **naïve** to believe that all of the students would hand in the work on time; her optimism was misplaced.

d) The home run that Adam hit in the fifth innings scored a triple leaving the opposing team completely **demoralized**.

e) The policeman suspected that the driver was drunk when his car began to **meander** across all three lanes of the highway.

f) It was rather **presumptuous** or **brazen** of Romeo to climbs up to Juliet's balcony, but he was in love.

g) The flame at the grave of President John F. Kennedy burns **perpetually**.

h) There had been no rain for years, and then it rained **incessantly** for three weeks.

i) The coach, a former professional, demanded more **resolve** and determination from the players at the tennis academy.

j) The teacher appeared to be **oblivious** to the taunting and bullying that went on in his classroom.

k) The proposed **induction** of Pete Rose into the Baseball Hall of Fame was once again defeated.

l) At the talent show, Rory **sauntered** up to the microphone as though he had no nerves at all.

m) The kicker watched with mounting **anguish** or **consternation** as the game-winning conversion went wide.

n) The supposed relic was in face a forgery which the archeologist was **brazen** enough to present as genuine.

o) On the final lap of the one mile race, Roy's **resolve** finally evaporated as Katie blew past him in the back stretch.

p) The plan was certainly **ingenious** - perhaps it was just a little too clever.

To the Reader

Ray strives to make his products the best that they can be. If you have any comments or questions about this book *please* contact the author through his email: **moore.ray1@yahoo.com**

Visit his website at **http://www.raymooreauthor.com**

Also by Ray Moore: Most books are available from amazon.com as paperbacks and at most online eBook retailers.

Fiction:

The Lyle Thorne Mysteries: each book features five tales from the Golden Age of Detection:

> *Investigations of The Reverend Lyle Thorne*
> *Further Investigations of The Reverend Lyle Thorne*
> *Early Investigations of Lyle Thorne*
> *Sanditon Investigations of The Reverend Lyle Thorne*
> *Final Investigations of The Reverend Lyle Thorne*

Non-fiction:

The *Critical Introduction series* is written for high school teachers and students and for college undergraduates. Each volume gives an in-depth analysis of a key text:

> *"The Stranger" by Albert Camus: A Critical Introduction* (Revised Second Edition)
> *"The General Prologue" by Geoffrey Chaucer: A Critical Introduction*
> *"Pride and Prejudice" by Jane Austen: A Critical Introduction*
> *"The Great Gatsby" by F. Scott Fitzgerald: A Critical Introduction*

The Text and Critical Introduction series differs from the Critical introduction series as these books contain the original medieval text together with an interlinear translation to aid the understanding of the text. The commentary allows the reader to develop a deeper understanding of the text and themes within the text.

> *"Sir Gawain and the Green Knight": Text and Critical Introduction*
> *"The General Prologue" by Geoffrey Chaucer: Text and Critical Introduction*
> *"The Wife of Bath's Prologue and Tale" by Geoffrey Chaucer: Text and Critical Introduction*
> *"Heart of Darkness" by Joseph Conrad: Text and Critical Introduction*
> *"The Sign of Four" by Sir Arthur Conan Doyle Text and Critical Introduction*

Study guides available in print- listed alphabetically by author

> * denotes also available as an eBook
> *"Wuthering Heights" by Emily Brontë: A Study Guide* *
> *"Jane Eyre" by Charlotte Brontë: A Study Guide* *
> *"The Meursault Investigation" by Kamel Daoud: A Study Guide*

"Great Expectations" by Charles Dickens: A Study Guide *
"The Myth of Sisyphus" and "The Stranger" by Albert Camus: Two Study Guides *
"The Sign of Four" by Sir Arthur Conan Doyle: A Study Guide *
"A Room with a View" by E. M. Forster: A Study Guide
"On the Road" by Jack Keruoac: A Study Guide
"An Inspector Calls" by J.B. Priestley: A Study Guide
"Macbeth" by William Shakespeare: A Study Guide *
"Othello" by William Shakespeare: A Study Guide *
"Antigone" by Sophocles: A Study Guide *
"Oedipus Rex" by Sophocles: A Study Guide
"Cannery Row" by John Steinbeck: A Study Guide
"Of Mice and Men" by John Steinbeck: A Study Guide *

Study Guides available as e-books:
"Heart of Darkness" by Joseph Conrad: A Study Guide
"The Mill on the Floss" by George Eliot: A Study Guide
"Lord of the Flies" by William Golding: A Study Guide
"Catch-22" by Joseph Heller: A Study Guide
"Life of Pi" by Yann Martel: A Study Guide
"Nineteen Eighty-Four by George Orwell: A Study Guide
"Selected Poems" by Sylvia Plath: A Study Guide
"Henry IV Part 2" by William Shakespeare: A Study Guide
"Julius Caesar" by William Shakespeare: A Study Guide
"The Pearl" by John Steinbeck: A Study Guide
"Slaughterhouse-Five" by Kurt Vonnegut: A Study Guide
"The Bridge of San Luis Rey" by Thornton Wilder: A Study Guide

Teacher resources: Ray also publishes many more study guides and other resources for classroom use on the 'Teachers Pay Teachers' website: **http://www.teacherspayteachers.com/Store/Raymond-Moore**

45768136R00024

Made in the USA
Middletown, DE
13 July 2017